THE
UNITED STATES
BOOKS

SOUTH DAKOTA

PICTURE BOOK OF

SOUTH DAKOTA

REVISED EDITION

By

BERNADINE BAILEY

Pictures by
KURT WIESE

ALBERT WHITMAN AND COMPANY
CHICAGO   ILLINOIS

Published simultaneously
in the Dominion of Canada
by George J. McLeod, Ltd., Toronto

© by Albert Whitman & Company, 1966, 1960
Library of Congress Catalog Card
Number 60-11569
Lithographed in the U.S.A.

SOUTH DAKOTA

RING-NECKED PHEASANT

NORTH DAKOTA

MONTANA

Grand R.

Moreau R.

MOBRIDGE

Oahe Reservoir

ABERDEEN

SISSETON

Lake Traverse

Big Stone Lake

MILBANK

MINNE

Belle Fourche Reservoir

BELLE FOURCHE

Cheyenne R.

WATERTOWN

SPEARFISH

Belle Fourche R.

STURGIS

DEADWOOD

LEAD

VILLA RANCHAERO

BLACK HILLS

RAPID CITY

Mount Rushmore Nat'l Mem.

Harney Peak

Badlands Nat'l Mon.

Jewel Cave Nat'l Mon.

Wind Cave Nat'l Park

HOT SPRINGS

Angostura Reservoir

PIERRE

Lake Sharpe

Big Bend Dam

White R.

WINNER

Lake Francis Case

HURON

BROOKINGS

MADISON

MITCHELL

SIOUX FALLS

James R.

Big Sioux R.

IOWA

WYOMING

NEBRASKA

Missouri R.

YANKTON

VERMILLION

Lewis and Clark Lake

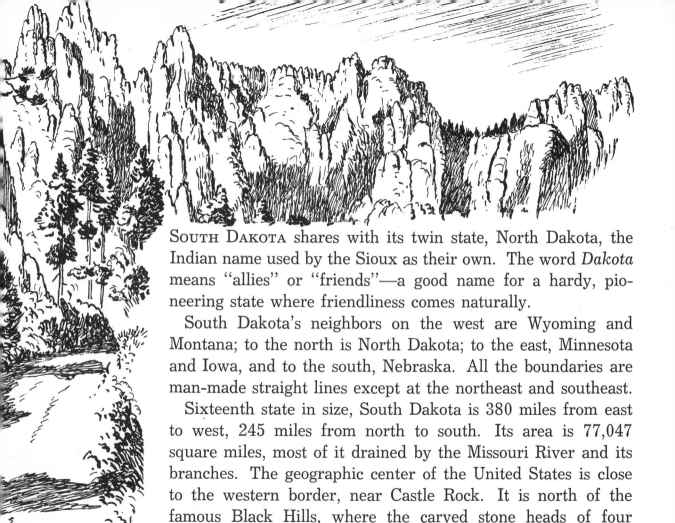

South Dakota shares with its twin state, North Dakota, the Indian name used by the Sioux as their own. The word *Dakota* means "allies" or "friends"—a good name for a hardy, pioneering state where friendliness comes naturally.

South Dakota's neighbors on the west are Wyoming and Montana; to the north is North Dakota; to the east, Minnesota and Iowa, and to the south, Nebraska. All the boundaries are man-made straight lines except at the northeast and southeast.

Sixteenth state in size, South Dakota is 380 miles from east to west, 245 miles from north to south. Its area is 77,047 square miles, most of it drained by the Missouri River and its branches. The geographic center of the United States is close to the western border, near Castle Rock. It is north of the famous Black Hills, where the carved stone heads of four great Presidents look down from the side of Mount Rushmore.

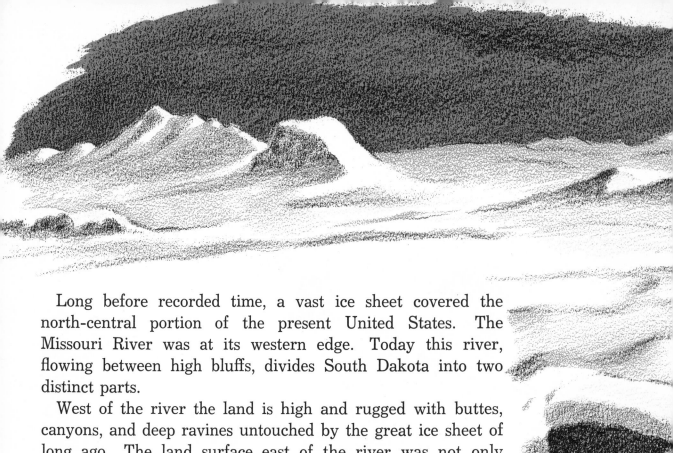

Long before recorded time, a vast ice sheet covered the north-central portion of the present United States. The Missouri River was at its western edge. Today this river, flowing between high bluffs, divides South Dakota into two distinct parts.

West of the river the land is high and rugged with buttes, canyons, and deep ravines untouched by the great ice sheet of long ago. The land surface east of the river was not only leveled by the thick ice, it was given a deep covering of rich soil called loess. When the ice melted, it left a gently sloping plain drained by the James, Vermillion, and Big Sioux rivers. These rivers flow south to join the Missouri.

Eastern South Dakota is dotted with lakes and marshes. The biggest lakes are man-made reservoirs formed by dams along the Missouri and its tributaries. The "Great Lakes of South Dakota" were formed by four dams along the Missouri. Besides preventing floods, these dams generate almost seventy per cent of the state's electric power.

Because the sun shines here almost every day, South Dakota is often called the Sunshine State. Although the temperatures can go to great extremes, the climate is usually moderate with low humidity. Rainfall is heaviest in the southeast, where it measures about 25 inches annually.

The first explorers came in 1743. Two French-Canadians, the La Vérendrye brothers, came to the present site of Fort Pierre and claimed it for France. As proof, they engraved a lead plate, buried it in the ground, and marked the place with a pile of stones. The plate was uncovered in 1913, over a century and a half later.

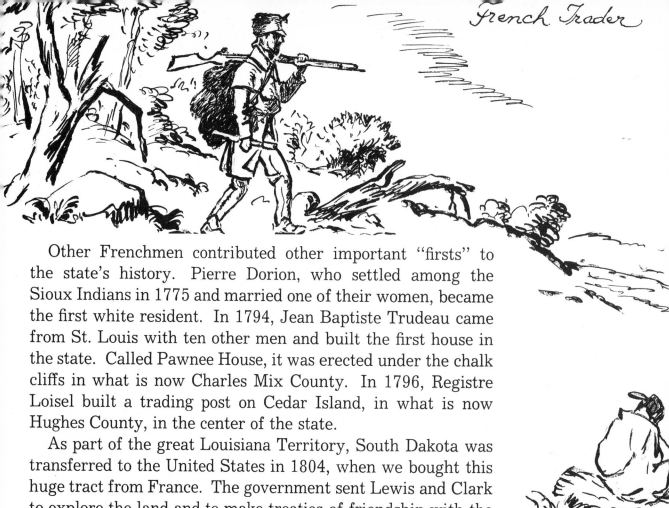

French Trader

Other Frenchmen contributed other important "firsts" to the state's history. Pierre Dorion, who settled among the Sioux Indians in 1775 and married one of their women, became the first white resident. In 1794, Jean Baptiste Trudeau came from St. Louis with ten other men and built the first house in the state. Called Pawnee House, it was erected under the chalk cliffs in what is now Charles Mix County. In 1796, Registre Loisel built a trading post on Cedar Island, in what is now Hughes County, in the center of the state.

As part of the great Louisiana Territory, South Dakota was transferred to the United States in 1804, when we bought this huge tract from France. The government sent Lewis and Clark to explore the land and to make treaties of friendship with the Indians.

8

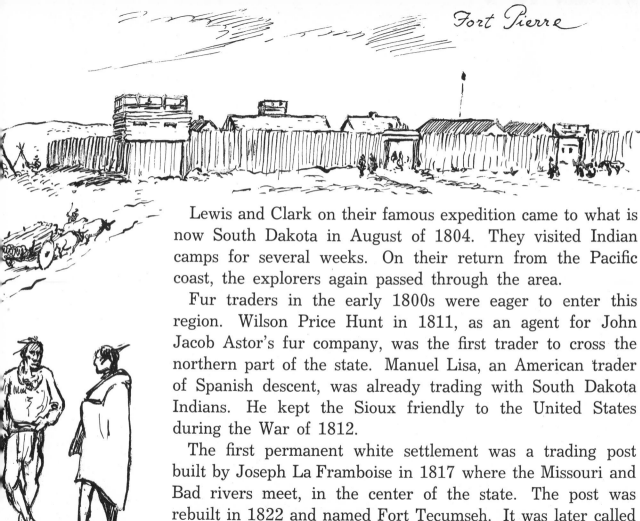

Fort Pierre

Lewis and Clark on their famous expedition came to what is now South Dakota in August of 1804. They visited Indian camps for several weeks. On their return from the Pacific coast, the explorers again passed through the area.

Fur traders in the early 1800s were eager to enter this region. Wilson Price Hunt in 1811, as an agent for John Jacob Astor's fur company, was the first trader to cross the northern part of the state. Manuel Lisa, an American trader of Spanish descent, was already trading with South Dakota Indians. He kept the Sioux friendly to the United States during the War of 1812.

The first permanent white settlement was a trading post built by Joseph La Framboise in 1817 where the Missouri and Bad rivers meet, in the center of the state. The post was rebuilt in 1822 and named Fort Tecumseh. It was later called Fort Pierre Chouteau, and finally Fort Pierre.

9

The journey up the Missouri River by the steamer "Yellowstone" in 1831 to Fort Pierre marked the beginning of a new era in the fur trade. A trip that once took months was covered in a few weeks. The fur trade boomed until the War Between the States. Then the decrease in the number of fur-bearing animals and growing Indian troubles brought the trade to an end.

Treaties in 1851 and 1858 with the Sioux Indians opened land between the Missouri and the Big Sioux rivers to settlement. The Indians were sent to the Yankton Reservation, further west. Yankton remains today one of the state's six Indian reservations.

10

The towns of Bon Homme, Yankton, and Vermillion grew up as trading centers for the farmers who had homesteaded land nearby. The first school house in South Dakota was built in Bon Homme, in 1860. With log walls and a dirt floor, the school had ten pupils during its three-month term. The first church, of Presbyterian denomination, was built in Vermillion, also in 1860.

On March 2, 1861, President Buchanan signed the bill creating the Dakota Territory. It included what is now North and South Dakota, along with the eastern portions of Montana and Wyoming. In this huge area there were only 2,402 white people. Dr. William Jayne, of Springfield, Illinois, was appointed governor, and he selected Yankton as the capital.

The pioneers faced Indian attacks and plagues of grasshoppers. A railroad built in 1871 to Gary, on the eastern border, and later from Elk Point and Yankton, on the southern border, made life a little easier.

The magic cry of "Gold!" began the big rush to the Black Hills. A military expedition under the leadership of General George A. Custer discovered gold near the present town of Custer on August 2, 1874. Next year, John B. Pearson found rich placer diggings between the present cities of Lead and Deadwood. By the summer of 1876, more than 25,000 people had come to seek their fortune in the hills. But by treaty, all of South Dakota west of the Missouri belonged to the Sioux. The Indians, led by Crazy Horse and Sitting Bull, fought desperately to keep their lands.

A new treaty with the Indians was signed in 1876. The Indians gave up their claims to the Black Hills and settled on reservations.

Lured by gold and free land, settlers continued to pour into the Dakota Territory. The great land rush lasted from 1878 to 1887. In that time, the Federal government granted 24,000,000 acres of public land to homesteaders and speculators. Railroads were built as far as the Missouri River by 1880, and many towns were founded east of the river. West of the Missouri, people had to travel by stage coach and ox train over rough trails.

After the formation of the Montana and Wyoming Territories, there was much talk of dividing Dakota Territory into two parts. North Dakota and South Dakota were admitted to the Union as separate states on the same day, November 2, 1889. Pierre was made the capital of the fortieth state.

A final struggle with the Indians came in 1890. The government feared that Sitting Bull was leading an uprising. He was killed resisting arrest. Cavalry troops overtook two hundred of his followers and massacred them at the Battle of Wounded Knee.

14

Pioneers who settled in South Dakota were interested in education. Seven years before statehood, the University of South Dakota was founded in Vermillion. The first college opened at Yankton in 1881.

In the 1890s drought and hard times slowed settlement. Then in the 1900s there was a rapid increase. From fewer than 12,000 people in 1870, the state grew to about 590,000 in 1910.

South Dakota is today mainly a farming state. More people work in agriculture than in any other occupation.

Life has not been easy for South Dakota farmers. Besides fighting off Indians and plowing under the buffalo grass that covered the prairies, they have had to work against drought, heat, dust storms, and hordes of grasshoppers. By using irrigation, land and forest conservation, terracing of hillsides, drainage, and dams, the land has been made productive. Wheat, corn, alfalfa, and flaxseed are among the leading crops.

In recent years, raising livestock has become more important than growing crops. In the western part of the state beef cattle graze on huge ranches. Young cattle are shipped to feedlots in eastern South Dakota where they are fattened for market. Dairy cattle are raised throughout the state. Creameries operate in Sioux Falls, Rapid City, Mitchell, and other cities.

The three northwestern counties are especially well suited to sheep raising. Here are good shelter, water, and plenty of space and natural grasses for pasture. Wool from the sheep of this area ranks with the best in the country. The spring lambs are shipped to many markets.

17

PIERRE
The Capitol

South Dakota is also a leading hog-raising state. Hogs are kept by farmers in the southeast where corn, alfalfa, and clover are grown for feed. Nearly every farmer in this section has chickens and turkeys. Poultry and eggs are the bases for food industries in several cities.

The capital, Pierre (pronounced "peer"), is almost exactly in the center of the state. Built on the east bank of the Missouri River, Pierre is a meeting place for western ranchers and eastern farmers, as well as for businessmen and government workers. Livestock and grain marketing and shipping are the main industries. The huge Oahe Dam is just north of the city. Southwest of Pierre is the new Big Bend Dam.

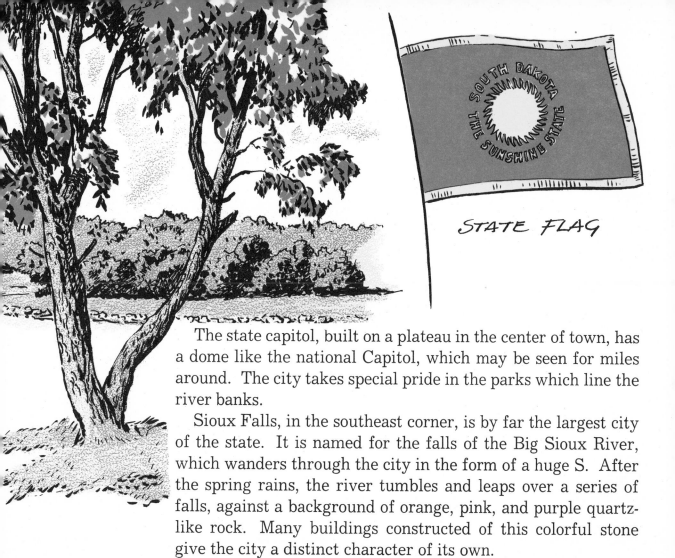

STATE FLAG

The state capitol, built on a plateau in the center of town, has a dome like the national Capitol, which may be seen for miles around. The city takes special pride in the parks which line the river banks.

Sioux Falls, in the southeast corner, is by far the largest city of the state. It is named for the falls of the Big Sioux River, which wanders through the city in the form of a huge S. After the spring rains, the river tumbles and leaps over a series of falls, against a background of orange, pink, and purple quartz-like rock. Many buildings constructed of this colorful stone give the city a distinct character of its own.

BACON SLABS
IN A SMOKE HOUSE

Farm products and livestock from the great agricultural area around Sioux Falls are brought to be processed, packed, and shipped out by truck and train.

An unusual industry at Sioux Falls is the manufacture of high-altitude balloons. The Pathfinder Atomic Power Plant near the city began production of electricity for commercial use in 1966.

Sioux Falls College, Augustana College, and North American Baptist Seminary are denominational colleges of high standing.

Rapid City, in the western part of the state, forms the eastern gateway to the Black Hills as well as a link between the northern and the southern hills. Named for Rapid Creek, which races eastward to the Missouri, Rapid City is the largest city west of the Missouri.

In Rapid City, one can find traces of the past as well as beautiful modern homes. A number of modern factories turn out cement, lumber, jewelry, saddles, flour, dairy products, meat, and tourist novelties.

President Coolidge's visit to the Black Hills in 1927 called national attention to this area as a vacation spot. Tourists also came to watch Gutzon Borglum carve the giant-size figures on Mount Rushmore. As a result, Rapid City has developed a large tourist business.

The South Dakota School of Mines and Technology and its Museum indicate the great part that mining has played in the growth of the entire state.

Aberdeen lies in the fertile valley of the James River, in the northeast part of the state. It is primarily a distributing rather than a manufacturing center. People come from as far as a hundred miles to shop in the retail stores, while the wholesale houses service much of the state, as well as parts of North Dakota and Montana.

23

In Aberdeen there are many people of Russian, German, and Scandinavian ancestry as well as others descended from pioneers from other states. Some church organizations still give dinners in old-country style, and wedding festivities may feature European customs.

At different times two well-known writers lived in Aberdeen. Hamlin Garland, who died in 1940, used South Dakota as the background for *Main Traveled Roads* and *A Son of the Middle Border*. Frank Baum, whose *Wizard of Oz* has amused many children, lived in Aberdeen as a young man and edited the weekly newspaper.

Huron, the key city in the James River Irrigation Project, was named for an Indian tribe. It is known to hunters as the pheasant capital of the United States. Thousands of sportsmen come here each fall, sure of finding game. Huron College was moved here from Pierre in 1898.

Mitchell, south of Huron on the James River, has two unusual attractions. The Corn Palace is decorated with murals made from corn and other grains for the September festival that climaxes the harvest season. Cowboy songs and Indian music are on tapes kept at the Sons of the Middle Border Museum. Dakota Wesleyan University is also located in Mitchell. There are meat-packing houses and creameries, and Mitchell is an important shipping point for livestock and grain.

Watertown, in the eastern part of the state, is on the Big Sioux River near Lake Kampeska. Many visitors come for fishing and swimming in the summer, hunting in the fall, and skating and iceboating in the winter.

Lead, (pronounced "leed") in the Black Hills National Forest, is famous for its Homestake Mine. Opened in 1878, in the days of the gold rush, this mine annually produces over $20,000,000 worth of gold. It is the greatest gold-producing mine in this hemisphere. The town's name comes from the mining term "lead" which refers to a vein of gold or other metal.

Other metals found in the Black Hills include iron, lead, oil, uranium, limestone, clay, gypsum, and bismuth.

26

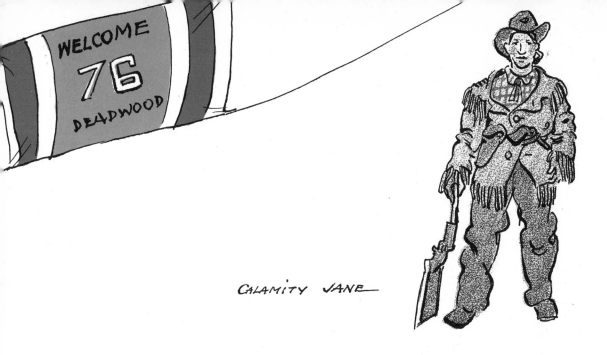

CALAMITY JANE

Deadwood, only three miles away, can also look back to the days of the gold rush. Such famous frontier characters as Wild Bill Hickok, Calamity Jane, Preacher Smith, and Seth Bullock are buried in Mt. Moriah cemetery.

During the first week of August, Deadwood revives the boom period of the gold rush in a three-day celebration called "Days of '76." Parades of covered wagons and stagecoaches, a rodeo, a pageant, and a performance of the trial of Jack McCall, who shot Wild Bill Hickok, bring back the gay days of long ago.

Sixty miles east of the beautiful Black Hills National Forest is a desolate area called the Badlands. It was named this long ago because no crop would grow on the poor soil, and travel was difficult. Now a national monument, the Badlands cover 250 square miles of land eroded by wind and water into strange shapes, many of them brightly colored. Sioux warriors once fought off army troops from high cliffs in the Badlands.

There is little animal life in the Badlands, but deeply buried in the earth, scientists have found bones of the saber-toothed tiger, dinosaurs, and the three-toed horse. In this quiet land where no one lives and no crop grows, the visitor can marvel at the mysteries of nature.

28

MODEL OF
THE MEMORIAL
TO THE AMERICAN
INDIAN.

THUNDER HEAD
MOUNTAIN IN
BACK.

Chief point of interest in the Black Hills is the 6,000-foot Mount Rushmore. The faces of four great Americans—George Washington, Thomas Jefferson, Abraham Lincoln, and Theodore Roosevelt—have been carved from the solid granite that forms the mountainside. For fourteen years, from 1927 to 1941, the great sculptor Gutzon Borglum worked on this world-famous memorial. Each likeness is about sixty feet from chin to forehead.

Another great sculptor, Korczak Ziolkowski of Boston, is carving an enormous monument on Thunderhead Mountain. When finished, it will be a huge statue of the Sioux Indian Chief, Crazy Horse, sitting on a racing horse.

Near Hot Springs is Wind Cave National Park. Its limestone cavern is filled with colorful crystal formations. Buffalo and other plains animals range through the park.

South Dakota's beautiful but rugged landscape and its pioneer days have been pictured in Ole Rölvaag's novel, *Giants of the Earth*. Rose Wilder Lane, born in De Smet, wrote of early hardships in *Let the Hurricane Roar*. Her mother, Laura Ingalls Wilder, is known for her series of children's books that begins with *Little House in the Big Woods*.

A modern pioneer from South Dakota—this time in science— is Ernest O. Lawrence, Nobel prize winner and inventor of the cyclotron.

INDEX

ILLUSTRATIONS